Trains on the Tracks

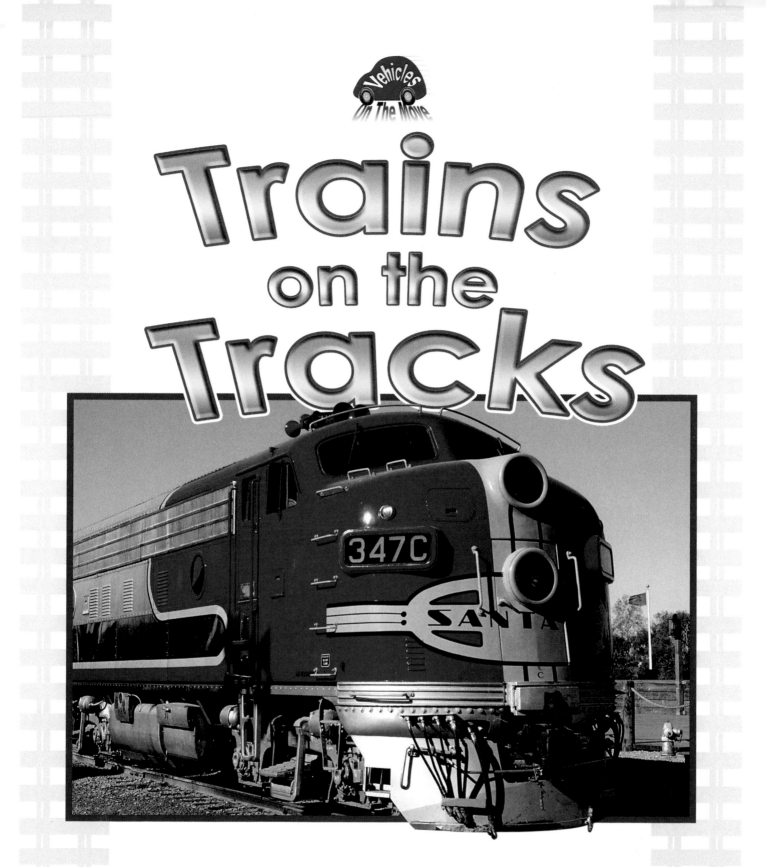

Kathryn Smithyman and Bobbie Kalman

🌳 Crabtree Publishing Company

www.crabtreebooks.com

Created by Bobbie Kalman

Dedicated by Bobbie Kalman
For our grandsons Sean and Liam (our two expert train engineers)

Editor-in-Chief
Bobbie Kalman

Writing team
Kathryn Smithyman
Bobbie Kalman

Substantive editor
Kelley MacAulay

Editors
Molly Aloian
Michael Hodge

Photo research
Crystal Foxton

Design
Margaret Amy Salter

Production coordinator
Heather Fitzpatrick

Prepress technician
Nancy Johnson

Consultant
Michael E. Telzrow, Executive Director
National Railroad Museum, Green Bay, Wisconsin

Special thanks to
Steve Cruickshanks (Ethan's train grandpa), Amtrak, a service mark of the National Railroad Passenger Corp. (U.S.), Canadian National Railway, and Canadian Pacific Railway

Illustrations
Vanessa Parson-Robbs: back cover, pages 7, 9, 11, 14, 16, 17, 18, 20, 24, 27, 32 (boxcar, freight train, gondola car, hopper car, locomotive, passenger train, and tank car)
Margaret Amy Salter: pages 21, 31, 32 (autorack, elevated train, flat car, passenger car, subway, and train station)

Photographs
Amtrak, a service mark of the National Railroad Passenger Corp. (U.S.): pages 13 (top), 28
Canadian Pacific Railway: pages 5, 23, 24-25, 29 (top)
CN: page 22
Corbis: © Colin Garratt, Milepost 92 1/2: page 7; © Jean Heguy: pages 18-19; Joseph Sohm: page 27
Fotolia.com: © Wai Heng Chow: page 26; © John Stelzer: page 31
iStockphoto.com: Aback Photography: page 6; Denise Kappa: page 21; James Pauls: page 11; Kenneth Sponsler: page 17
© WOLFGANG KAEHLER, www.wkaehlerphoto.com: page 29 (bottom)
© Marcel Marchon: page 30
© ShutterStock.com: Anita: pages 10, 20; Mariano N. Ruiz: pages 8-9
Other images by Corel

Library and Archives Canada Cataloguing in Publication

Smithyman, Kathryn
    Trains on the tracks / Kathryn Smithyman & Bobbie Kalman.

(Vehicles on the move)
Includes index.
ISBN 978-0-7787-3045-3 (bound)
ISBN 978-0-7787-3059-0 (pbk.)

    1. Railroad trains--Juvenile literature. I. Kalman, Bobbie, 1947- II. Title. III. Series.

TF148.S65 2007   j625.1   C2007-900946-8

Library of Congress Cataloging-in-Publication Data

Smithyman, Kathryn, 1961-
    Trains on the tracks / Kathryn Smithyman & Bobbie Kalman.
        p. cm. -- (Vehicles on the move)
    Includes index.
    ISBN-13: 978-0-7787-3045-3 (rlb)
    ISBN-10: 0-7787-3045-X (rlb)
    ISBN-13: 978-0-7787-3059-0 (pb)
    ISBN-10: 0-7787-3059-X (pb)
    1. Railroad trains--Juvenile literature. I. Kalman, Bobbie. II. Title.
TF148.S69 2007
625.2--dc22
                                                        2007005078

Crabtree Publishing Company

www.crabtreebooks.com   1-800-387-7650

Published in Canada
Crabtree Publishing
616 Welland Ave.
St. Catharines, Ontario
L2M 5V6

Published in the United States
Crabtree Publishing
PMB16A
350 Fifth Ave., Suite 3308
New York, NY 10118

Published in the United Kingdom
Crabtree Publishing
White Cross Mills
High Town, Lancaster
LA1 4XS

Published in Australia
Crabtree Publishing
386 Mt. Alexander Rd.
Ascot Vale (Melbourne)
VIC 3032

Contents

What is a train?

A **train** is a **vehicle**. A vehicle is a machine. Vehicles move from place to place. They move people and things. A train moves from place to place on **tracks**.

tracks

Parts of a train

A train has a **locomotive**. The locomotive has an **engine**. An engine gives the train **power**. Power makes the train move. A train also has **railcars**. The locomotive pulls the railcars.

railcar

locomotive

The locomotive is at the front of the train.

Train parts

Locomotives and railcars have parts called **knuckle couplers**. Knuckle couplers join railcars together. They also join railcars to locomotives.

knuckle coupler

Locomotives and railcars have knuckle couplers on their front ends. They also have knuckle couplers on their back ends.

Locomotive parts

Locomotives have parts that railcars do not have. They have **cabs**, **headlights**, and **horns**.

A locomotive's horn makes a loud noise. The noise tells people that the train is coming!

cab

Headlights are lights on the front of the locomotive. They help the driver of the train see the tracks ahead of the train.

fireman

engineer

*The driver of a train is called an **engineer**. The engineer sits on the right side of the cab. The **fireman** helps the engineer. The fireman sits on the left side of the cab.*

Train tracks

Trains travel on tracks. Most tracks have two **rails**. Rails are long, thin bars. They are made of **steel**. Steel is a kind of metal. Steel is strong and hard.

rail

Ties and spikes

Rails lie on top of **ties**. Most ties are pieces of wood. **Spikes** attach the rails to the ties. Spikes are long metal nails. The spikes hold the rails in place.

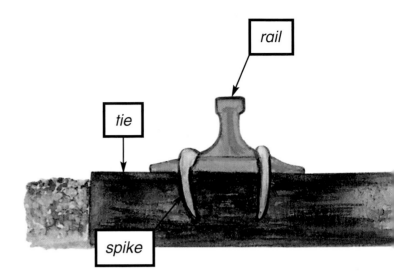

rail

tie

spike

tie

Tracks are laid on top of gravel called **ballast**.

Steel wheels

Trains move on **wheels**. The
wheels are on the locomotives
and the railcars. The wheels are
round. They are made of steel.

wheel

A perfect fit

Each train wheel has two **rims**.
A rim is the edge of a wheel.
One rim of a train wheel is larger
than the other rim is. The larger
rim is called a **flange**. The flange
holds the wheel firmly on the rail.

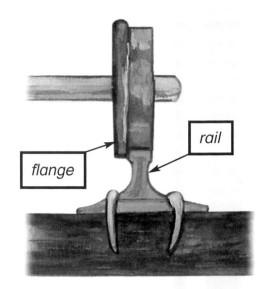

A flange stops a train wheel from slipping off the tracks.

Two kinds of trains

There are different kinds of trains. Most trains are **freight trains**. Freight trains carry **freight**. Freight is a load of things. Freight trains carry freight in railcars. Railcars that carry freight are called **freight cars**.

freight cars

Freight trains carry many kinds of freight. Wheat, logs, and new cars are kinds of freight.

Passenger trains

Some trains are **passenger trains**. These trains carry **passengers**. Passengers are people who are riding on trains. They ride in railcars called **passenger cars**.

Passenger cars have seats in them. People sit in the seats.

passenger car

Passenger cars have windows. The passengers can look out the windows.

Freight trains

Freight trains have large, powerful locomotives called **freight locomotives**. Freight locomotives can pull many freight cars filled with freight.

Pulling partners

Sometimes freight cars carry very heavy freight. One locomotive may not be able to pull these freight cars. Two or more locomotives can be joined together. Together, these locomotives can pull very heavy freight cars.

Four freight locomotives are pulling this freight train.

Tank cars and hopper cars

Different kinds of freight cars carry different kinds of freight. **Tank cars** are freight cars. They carry liquids. Each tank car carries a different liquid. Some tank cars carry milk. Other tank cars carry **gasoline**. Gasoline is the fuel that most vehicles use for power.

tank car

Hopper cars

A **hopper car** is another kind of freight car. It can carry huge loads of sand or gravel. There are doors in the floor of a hopper car. The doors open and close. When the doors open, the load pours out. It pours out into huge metal boxes. The boxes are below the tracks.

These hopper cars are holding freight. Their doors are closed.

Boxcars

Many freight cars are **boxcars**. Boxcars carry **packaged freight**. Packaged freight is freight that is wrapped in paper or plastic. Packaged freight may also be packed in boxes. Boxcars carry packaged freight such as canned foods, televisions, or books.

A boxcar is shaped like a box. It has a floor, four sides, and a roof. There are doors in the side of a boxcar. Freight is loaded in and out of the boxcar through the doors.

forklift

*Machines called **forklifts** move freight in and out of boxcars.*

Gondola cars and autoracks

A **gondola car** is another kind of freight car. It has four sides, but it does not have a roof. Gondola cars carry different kinds of freight. They may carry machine parts, scraps of metal, or logs.

These gondola cars are carrying logs.

Autoracks

Autoracks are freight cars that carry vehicles, such as cars, vans, and trucks. To load an autorack, people drive these vehicles up a **ramp** and into the autorack.

ramp

Each autorack holds about twenty vehicles.

Flatcars

Almost all freight trains have **flatcars**. Flatcars do not have walls or roofs. Flatcars carry machines, pipes, and wood. Some of the freight that flatcars carry is huge! Huge freight is too big to fit on other kinds of freight cars.

This flatcar is carrying huge pipes.

tank

This flatcar is carring a huge **tank**!

Passenger trains

Passenger trains carry people from place to place. Each passenger car carries a lot of people. Passenger cars weigh less than freight cars do. They also move faster than freight trains. Their locomotives have less weight to pull.

At the station

Passenger trains travel to **train stations**.
People get on trains at one train station.
They get off trains at another train station.
At train stations, there are buildings where
people wait for trains to arrive.

*People wait for trains on **platforms**. Trains stop next to the platforms.*

Ticket to ride

People can buy **tickets** at train stations. Each person must have a ticket to ride on a train. A **conductor** checks each passenger's ticket. The conductor checks to make sure each passenger is on the right train.

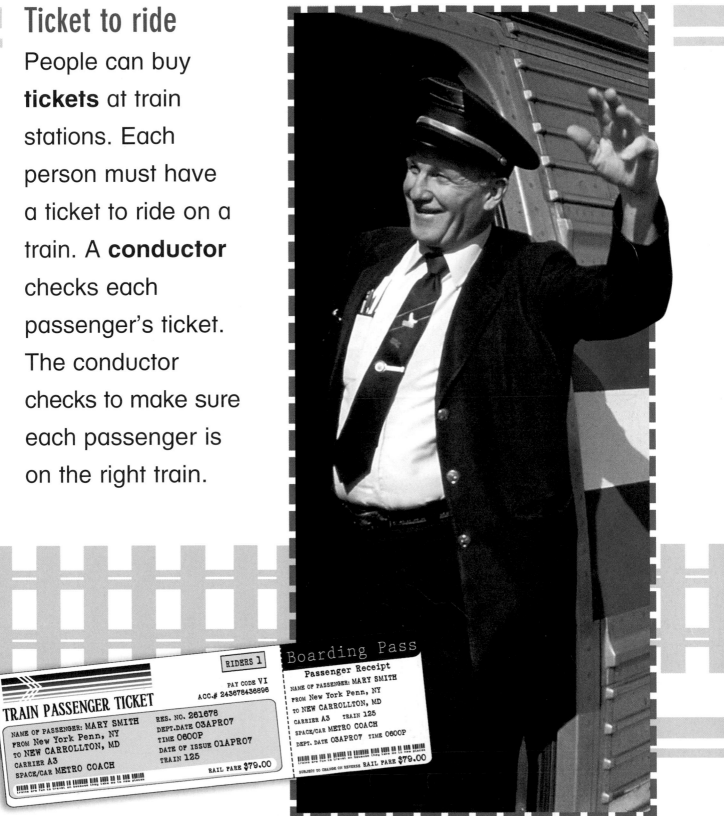

This conductor has checked all the passengers' tickets.

Traveling long distances

Some passengers travel very long distances on trains. Traveling long distances may take days. On a long trip, passengers need places to eat and sleep. Passenger trains that carry people long distances have special cars. These pages show some of the special cars.

*Passengers eat meals in the **dining car**.*

Passengers can sleep in a **sleeping car**. The sleeping car has beds called **berths**.

An **observation car** has large windows in its sides and roof. Passengers in the observation car can see mountains, lakes, and other beautiful sights from the train.

Commuter trains

Commuter trains are passenger trains on which people travel every day. Passengers take the trains to work, to school, or to other places they need to go.

Subways

Most large cities have **subways**. Subways are commuter trains that travel under the ground.

Elevated trains

Some cities have commuter trains called **elevated trains**. Elevated trains travel on tracks high above the ground.

Elevated trains are sometimes called "els."

Words to know and Index

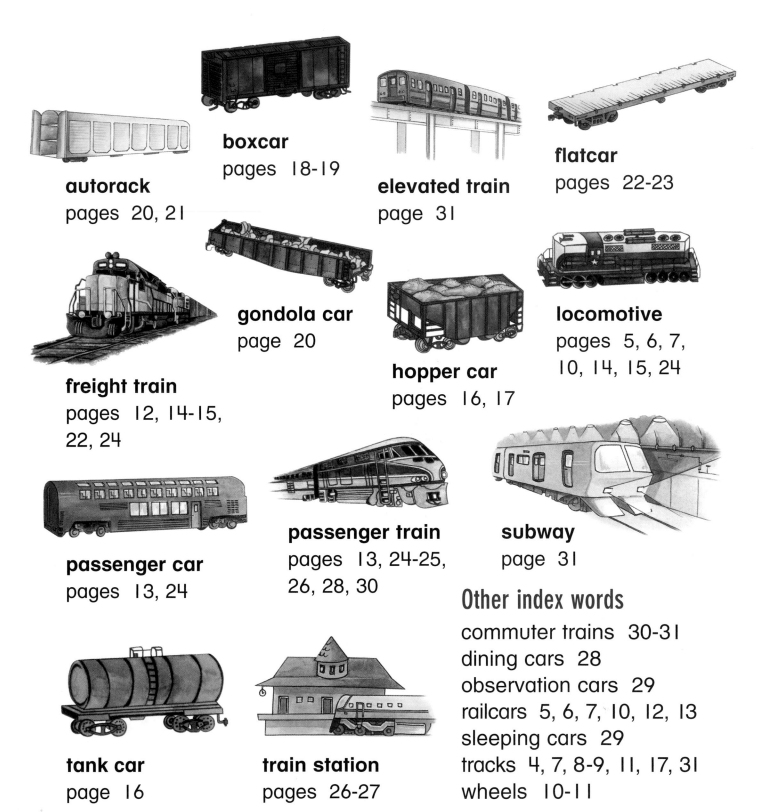

autorack
pages 20, 21

boxcar
pages 18-19

elevated train
page 31

flatcar
pages 22-23

freight train
pages 12, 14-15, 22, 24

gondola car
page 20

hopper car
pages 16, 17

locomotive
pages 5, 6, 7, 10, 14, 15, 24

passenger car
pages 13, 24

passenger train
pages 13, 24-25, 26, 28, 30

subway
page 31

tank car
page 16

train station
pages 26-27

Printed in the USA